BUCKINGHAM PALACE

HIS MAJESTY THE KING'S DECLARATION UPON HIS ACCESSION

Following the passing of Her Majesty Queen Elizabeth II, the Accession Council took place on Saturday 10 September 2022. The gathering of Privy Counsellors was broadcast on television for the first time in history. His Majesty King Charles III joined his first Privy Council meeting to deliver a personal declaration.

My Lords, Ladies, and Gentlemen.

It is my most sorrowful duty to announce to you the death of my beloved Mother, The Queen.

I know how deeply you, the entire Nation – and I think I may say the whole world – sympathise with me in the irreparable loss we have all suffered. It is the greatest consolation to me to know of the sympathy expressed by so many to my Sister and Brothers and that such overwhelming affection and support should be extended to our whole family in our loss.

To all of us as a family, as to this kingdom and the wider family of nations of which it is a part, my Mother gave an example of lifelong love and of selfless service. My Mother's reign was unequalled in its duration, its dedication and its devotion. Even as we grieve, we give thanks for this most faithful life.

I am deeply aware of this great inheritance and of the duties and heavy responsibilities of Sovereignty which have now passed to me. In taking up these responsibilities, I shall strive to follow the inspiring example I have been set in upholding constitutional government and to seek the peace, harmony and prosperity of the peoples of these Islands and of the Commonwealth Realms and Territories throughout the world.

In this purpose, I know that I shall be upheld by the affection and loyalty of the peoples whose Sovereign I have been called upon to be, and that in the discharge of these duties I will be guided by the counsel of their elected parliaments. In all this, I am profoundly encouraged by the constant support of my beloved wife.

I take this opportunity to confirm my willingness and intention to continue the tradition of surrendering the hereditary revenues, including the Crown Estate, to My Government for the benefit of all, in return for the Sovereign Grant, which supports My official duties as Head of State and Head of Nation.

And in carrying out the heavy task that has been laid upon me, and to which I now dedicate what remains to me of my life, I pray for the guidance and help of Almighty God.

Charles R.

WE ARE PROUD TO FLY THE FLAG WITH YOU

Your Majesties, we send our warmest wishes and congratulations on your Coronation.

It is an honour to serve you and we look forward to continuing to fly the flag with you.

THE CORONATION OF HIS MAJESTY KING CHARLES III AND HER MAJESTY QUEEN CAMILLA

OFFICIAL SOUVENIR PROGRAMME

SUPPORTING OUR CHARITY PARTNERS

SSAFA - The Armed Forces Charity

SSAFA, the Armed Forces charity, has been providing practical, emotional, and financial support to our Forces and their families since 1885 and not just during times of conflict. Our teams of volunteers and employees help those currently serving, veterans, and their families to retain their independence and dignity.

Royal Collection Trust

Royal Collection Trust looks after the Royal Collection, one of the most important art collections in the world, and manages the public opening of the official residences of His Majesty The King. Through our work, from exhibitions and learning programmes to publications and retail products, we aim to ensure that the Royal Collection and Palaces are valued and enjoyed by everyone.

PUBLICATIONS UK

The Official Souvenir Programme of The Coronation of His Majesty King Charles III and Her Majesty Queen Camilla is published by Publications UK for and on behalf of the Royal Household. Telephone: +44 (0)20 8238 5023. Website: *www.publicationsuk.co.uk*

PROGRAMME EDITOR	PUBLISHER & MANAGING DIRECTOR	PROGRAMME DESIGN	ADVERTISING PRODUCTION	SUB EDITOR	ROYAL HOUSEHOLD
Tom Corby MVO	*Stewart Lee*	*David Hicks*	*Angela Brown*	*Justyn Barnes*	*Poppy Izzard*

PICTURE CREDITS

The publisher and its partners are grateful for permission to reproduce the items listed below:

Cover © *Chris Jackson/Getty Images*; Page 2 © *Alexi Lubomirski*; Pages 6-7 *by Hannah McKay/ Alamy*; Pages 8-9 *by Jack Hill/The Times/Alamy & by Everett Collection/Alamy*; Pages 10-11/15 *Getty Images*; Pages 12-13 *by Chronicle/Alamy*; Page 14 *Alamy*; Page 16 *by Malcolm Park/Alamy*;

Page 18 *by Paul Grover/Alamy*; Page 19 *by Chris Jackson/WENN/AFF/Alamy*; Page 22/24 *Alamy*; Pages 14/32/42-43/44-45/46/48-49/51* © Royal Collection Trust*/© *His Majesty King Charles III 2023*; Pages 29/34/36/38/40/47 *Alamy*; Pages 33/35/36/38/40 © *The Dean and Chapter of Westminster*;

Page 50 *by Dorothy Wilding* © *William Hustler and Georgina Hustler / National Portrait Gallery, London*; Page 53 *by Hugo Burnand, Camera Press*; Page 54 *by Chris Jackson/Getty Images*; Pages 56-57 © *Buckingham Palace via Getty Images*; Page 58 *Alamy*; Page 59 *by Hugo Burnand/Alamy*;

Page 60 *by Ranald Mackechnie, Camera Press*; Pages 61/62-63/64-65 *Alamy*; 66-67 *by Arthur Edwards/ Alamy*; Page 68 *Shutterstock*; Pages 68-69/72 *Alamy/*; Page 71 *by Julian Calder/Camera Press*; Page 73 *Getty Images/Popperfoto*; Pages 75/76-77/78/80* © Royal Collection Trust/*© *His Majesty King Charles III 2023*.

THE ACCESSION
LONG LIVE THE KING

The accession of The King followed immediately after the passing of his mother. There was no pause. Such is the accession of our monarchs.

6

'IT WAS THE MOMENT I have been dreading', His Majesty The King told the then Prime Minister, Liz Truss, when he received her at Buckingham Palace. He was referring to the death of his mother, barely 24 hours earlier. It was a time of sadness for a deeply thoughtful man as he stepped into the role held by Britain's longest reigning, much-loved and globally admired monarch.

Below: Their Majesties King Charles III and Queen Camilla during the Accession Council.

Outside, there were crowds at the Palace gates and flags were flying at half-mast. The King spoke of this moment of great sadness and how he and his family profoundly mourned the passing of a cherished sovereign and much-loved mother. Later, His Majesty said he had been 'deeply touched' by the many messages he had received and by the expressions of support from the country and across the world. In an address to Parliament he said he 'felt the weight of history', vowing to emulate his mother's example of dutiful service.

The King's reign could hardly have got off to a better start. His well-judged speeches and his public appearances showed that the Crown remains a source of unity. The genuine outpouring of public support for His Majesty and for the institution of monarchy itself was testimony to the dignity with which The King successfully navigated the weeks following his accession. He has set out the guiding principles of his reign and has committed himself to respecting Britain's constitutional arrangements. His performance so far augurs well for the future, himself, his family and all of us. ✦

TOM CORBY MVO

The King and The Prince of Wales watch over the coffin of Her Majesty Queen Elizabeth II as it is carried out of Westminster Abbey.

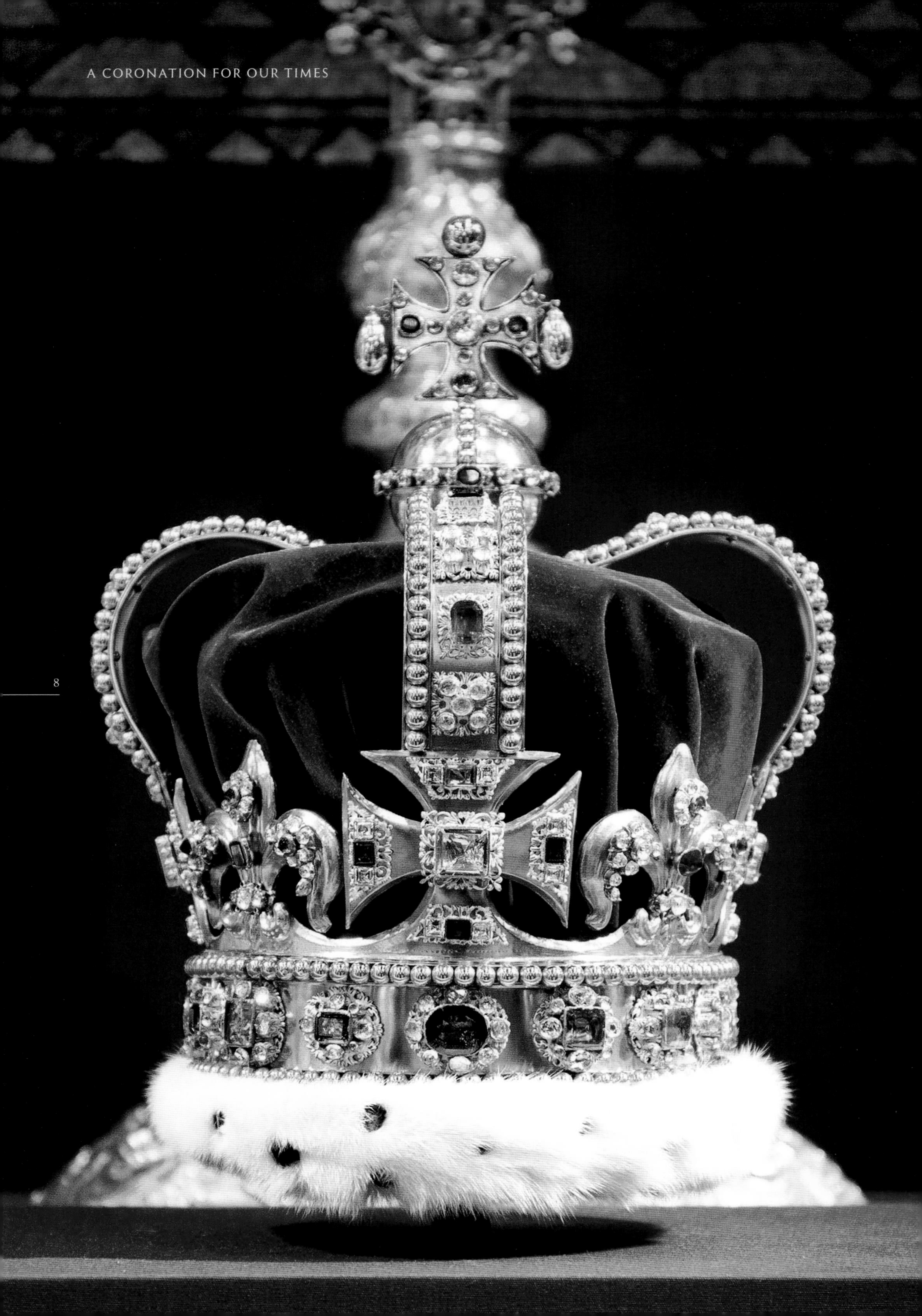

A CORONATION
FOR OUR TIMES

The eyes of the world will be on the Coronation of King Charles III. It promises to be an occasion of splendour and a fitting showcase for the United Kingdom.

THREE DAYS OF CELEBRATION in May will mark the Coronation of King Charles III. The Coronation will be conducted by the Archbishop of Canterbury and enacted in Westminster Abbey, scene of the coronations of our sovereigns for the past 900 years, dating back to that of William the Conqueror.

The crowning of the monarch is a ceremony rich in religious significance and pageantry. The starting point is Buckingham Palace, from where The King and The Queen will travel to Westminster Abbey. They will be accompanied by the Sovereign's Escort of the Household Cavalry. Other detachments from the Household Division will be on parade and the route will be a blaze of colour.

While being rooted in longstanding traditions, the Coronation ceremony will also reflect The King's role in modern Britain and look towards the future. It will be a time of inclusive celebration for the nation, the Commonwealth and His Majesty's Realms.

The ceremony has six phases: the Recognition, the Oath, the Anointing, the Investiture, which includes the Crowning, the Enthronement, and the Homage. ›

Opposite: St Edward's Crown is the crown historically used at the moment of crowning, and was worn by Her Majesty Queen Elizabeth II at her coronation in 1953.

Right: Queen Elizabeth II during her coronation ceremony.

The King will be annointed, blessed and consecrated by the Archbishop and the Dean of Westminster.

THE RECOGNITION

The Recognition dates back to Anglo-Saxon times. King Charles will stand in the space known as the Theatre and then will show himself 'unto the people', to the east, south, west and north.

Each time the Archbishop of Canterbury and others shall say to the people: 'I here present unto you King Charles, your undoubted King.' The people will then respond with loud and repeated acclamations.

THE CORONATION OATH

The King will then make the Coronation Oath undertaking to rule according to law, and to exercise justice with mercy – promises symbolised by the four swords in the regalia: the Sword of State, the two Swords of Justice and the blunt Sword of Mercy. He will also promise to maintain the Church of England.

THE ANOINTING

For the Anointing, The King will sit in King Edward's Chair, surrounded on three sides by an anointing screen. He will then be anointed, blessed and consecrated by the Archbishop of Canterbury and the Dean of Westminster using the Ampulla and the Anointing Spoon. The Ampulla holds the consecrated oil used to anoint the sovereign and takes the form of an eagle from whose beak the oil is poured. The Anointing Spoon is the most ancient treasure of the Coronation Regalia, dating back to the 12th century. It is one of the only pieces of the original regalia to survive the rule of Oliver Cromwell, who melted down most of it in 1649 after the execution of Charles I.

The Anointing is the central act of the religious ceremony and during it the choir sings the anthem 'Zadok the Priest', set to music by Handel for the coronation of George II, in 1727. It will be a solemn moment for The King who, having been sanctified, is ready for his Investiture with the ornaments that are the outward and visible signs of spiritual grace. >

THE BLESSING OF THE CORONATION OIL

For the first time in the history of the monarchy, the oil that will be used to anoint The King has been blessed outside the United Kingdom. The oil has been consecrated at the Church of the Holy Sepulchre in Jerusalem. In contrast, the oils used at the coronations of Edward VII, George VI and Elizabeth II were blessed in the Chapel of St Edward the Confessor in Westminster Abbey. The decision to use oil consecrated in Jerusalem, taken by the Archbishop of Canterbury in consultation with The King, reflects the association between the Coronation, the Bible and the Holy Land. It is also a tribute to Prince Philip, whose mother Princess Alice of Greece is buried in Jerusalem, on the Mount of Olives. Princess Alice wished for her own grave to be near that of her aunt, the Grand Duchess Elizabeth, who was recognised as a saint by the Russian Orthodox Church in 1984.

THE CORONATION OF HIS MAJESTY KING CHARLES III AND HER MAJESTY QUEEN CAMILLA

The assembly stands at the
moment of crowning, at the
coronation of Queen Elizabeth II.

12

The newly crowned King Charles III and
Queen Camilla will return to Buckingham Palace
in procession, and make an appearance on the
balcony in front of thousands of well-wishers.

*The culminating moment of
the ceremony is the Crowning.
The entire assembly will stand
as the Archbishop raises
St Edward's Crown which is
then placed on The King's head.*

THE INVESTITURE

First, The King will put on a sleeveless white
garment and then a cloth of gold robe. The King
is then presented with the Golden Spurs (the
symbol of chivalry), a jewelled sword and then
the Armills, the golden bracelets of sincerity
and wisdom. The King is dressed in the Imperial
Mantle and Stole Royal before receiving the
Sovereign's Orb and the Coronation Ring.
He also receives the Glove, a symbol of dignity
and his duty to give his blood for the sake of his
people, before receiving the Sovereign's Sceptre
and Rod, representing kingly power and justice,
and peace, respectively.

THE CROWNING

The culminating moment of the ceremony is the
Crowning. The entire assembly will stand as the
Archbishop raises St Edward's Crown which is
then placed on The King's head. Bells will ring
out and gun salutes will fire.

THE ENTHRONEMENT AND THE HOMAGE

The King is then enthroned and receives the
Homage of the Archbishop of Canterbury,
and The Prince of Wales, who swear their
fealty, and the Benediction, consisting of
prayers publicly affirmed by the congregation.
The Queen will then be invested, anointed,
crowned and enthroned. Prayers are said for
Their Majesties who receive Holy Communion.

The spiritual ceremony over, The King and
The Queen will then withdraw to St Edward's
Chapel, and The King will put on the Imperial
State Crown. Their Majesties will dress in the
Robes of Estate for the procession back to
Buckingham Palace and subsequent balcony
appearance with members of the Royal Family. ✦

A CROWN FOR THE QUEEN

Queen Camilla will wear Queen Mary's crown made for the coronation of
George V. It will be fitted with three Cullinan diamonds in tribute to the late
Queen Elizabeth II. The three most recent queen consorts – Alexandra, wife of
Edward VII; Mary, wife of George V; and Elizabeth, wife of George VI – had
crowns specially made for their coronations. Her Majesty's choice has been
described as 'a crown for a more conscious age'.

A CORONATION FOR THE PEOPLE

When Queen Elizabeth II was crowned in 1953, the coronation was televised for the first time. Some 27 million people in the United Kingdom, and millions more across the Commonwealth and around the world, watched the ceremony.

15

Soldiers of the Household Cavalry
ride down The Mall on 25 May 2019.

THE CORONATION OF HIS MAJESTY KING CHARLES III AND HER MAJESTY QUEEN CAMILLA

MOËT & CHANDON

MOËT & CHANDON OFFERS BEST WISHES TO THEIR MAJESTIES
THE KING AND THE QUEEN CONSORT ON THE OCCASION OF
THE CORONATION OF KING CHARLES III ON 6TH MAY 2023

THE MUSIC OF THE CORONATION

Westminster Abbey will hear glorious music from across the United Kingdom and the Commonwealth as The King and The Queen are crowned on 6 May.

Opposite: The choir at Westminster Abbey. *Top:* Alis Huws, official Royal Harpist. *Middle:* Lord Andrew Lloyd Webber. *Above:* Soprano Pretty Yende.

THE PROGRAMME will feature a variety of musical styles and performers, blending tradition, heritage and ceremony with new musical voices of today to reflect The King's lifelong love and support of music and the arts.

His Majesty has personally commissioned new music and selected the musical programme. Andrew Nethsingha, Organist and Master of the Choristers at Westminster Abbey, will be overseeing all musical arrangements and directing the music during the service.

Sir Antonio Pappano, Music Director of the Royal Opera House, will be conducting the Coronation Orchestra, which comprises a bespoke collection of musicians drawn from orchestras of The former Prince of Wales's patronages, including the Royal Philharmonic Orchestra.

A total of 12 new commissions – six orchestral commissions, five choral commissions and one organ commission – have been specially composed for the occasion by world-renowned British composers in classical, sacred, film, television, and musical theatre genres. The commissioned works include a new Coronation Anthem by Lord Andrew Lloyd Webber, a Coronation March by Patrick Doyle and a new commission for organ by Iain Farrington, embracing musical themes from countries across the Commonwealth. New works by composers including Sarah Class, Shirley J. Thompson and Judith Weir will also feature.

Soloists performing on the day will include the baritone Roderick Williams and the soprano Pretty Yende.

The official Royal Harpist Alis Huws will perform as part of the Coronation Orchestra in recognition of The King's deeply held relationship and affiliation with Wales. One of the liturgical sections of the ceremony will also be performed in Welsh.

Greek Orthodox music will be performed by the Byzantine Chant Ensemble in tribute to The King's late father, His Royal Highness The Prince Philip, who was a Prince of Greece and Denmark before taking British nationality.

British composers dating from the 16th century, who have historically featured in the coronation service over the centuries, will be included in the programme. Fanfares will also be played by the State Trumpeters of the Household Cavalry and the Fanfare Trumpeters of the Royal Air Force, and a gospel choir will also perform. ✦

THE CORONATION EMBLEM

The Coronation Emblem – which will feature throughout May's historic celebrations – combines iconic flora from each of the Home Nations to reflect The King's love of the natural world.

A CORONATION EMBLEM has been created to usher in the Carolean era. The emblem symbolises and celebrates the historic beginning of the new reign of King Charles III.

Using the red, white and blue of the Union Flag, the emblem pays tribute to The King's love of the natural world. It features the natural flora of the four nations of the United Kingdom – the rose of England, the thistle of Scotland, the daffodil of Wales and the shamrock of Northern Ireland. These flowers are elegantly combined to create the shape of St Edward's Crown.

The emblem will feature throughout the celebrations in May, including the Coronation service at Westminster Abbey and Coronation Concert at Windsor Castle, as well as national events, street parties and community gatherings.

The emblem will also be used for all official merchandise commemorating the Coronation of The King and The Queen, and will be seen across social media.

Created by Sir Jony Ive KBE, the internationally revered former Apple Chief Design Officer, and his creative collective LoveFrom, the emblem blends tradition with modernity and will become a familiar sight throughout May.

Speaking about the design of the emblem, Sir Jony said: 'It is such an honour to be able to contribute to this remarkable national occasion, and our team is very proud of this work. The design was inspired by His Majesty King Charles's love of the planet, nature, and his deep concern for the natural world.

'The emblem speaks to the happy optimism of spring and celebrates the beginning of this new Carolean era. The gentle modesty of these natural forms combine to define an emblem that acknowledges both the joy and profound importance of this occasion.' ✦

JAGUAR LAND ROVER

Jaguar Land Rover would like to extend its sincerest congratulations
to HM The King and HM The Queen Consort on this historic occasion.

The Coronation is a ceremony that brings us all together in celebration
and we very much look forward to continuing our support
for this new era of the Monarchy.

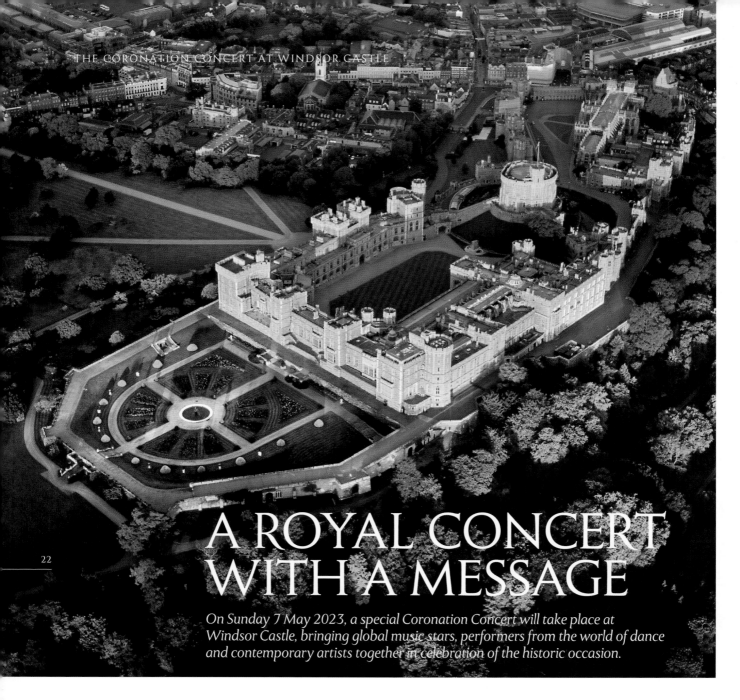

A ROYAL CONCERT WITH A MESSAGE

On Sunday 7 May 2023, a special Coronation Concert will take place at Windsor Castle, bringing global music stars, performers from the world of dance and contemporary artists together in celebration of the historic occasion.

THE ANCIENT WALLS of Windsor Castle will form the backdrop for the Coronation Concert, with volunteers from The King and The Queen's charities in the audience. A national ballot held by the BBC has allocated a pair of free tickets to 5,000 members of the public and the show will be broadcast live by the BBC.

The Coronation Concert will be full of joyful celebration and a memorable moment of the Coronation Weekend. Alongside stars of stage and screen, the Coronation Choir will exclusively perform on the night.

This wonderful choir has been created from the nation's keenest community choirs and amateur singers across the United Kingdom, including refugee choirs, NHS choirs, LGBTQ+ singing groups and deaf signing choirs. The Coronation Choir will appear alongside the Virtual Choir, made up of singers from across the Commonwealth, for a special performance on the night. A complementary documentary following the Coronation Choir's formation, telling the stories of the people representing the many faces and voices of the country, will also be screened.

The centrepiece of the Coronation Concert, Lighting up the Nation, will see the country join together in celebration as iconic locations across the United Kingdom are lit up using projections, lasers, drone displays and illuminations.

The Coronation Concert will be produced by BBC Studios and broadcast live on BBC One, BBC iPlayer, BBC Radio 2 and BBC Sounds. ✦

CROWN

It's not just paint,
it's personal.

from one Crown
to another,
congratulations
to Their Majesties
King Charles III and
The Queen Consort.

His Majesty The King meeting guests at The Big Lunch on the cricket pitch at The Oval, south London, in 2022.

24

CORONATION BIG LUNCH

The celebrations will also include the Coronation Big Lunch, reprising the Platinum Jubilee's street parties and encouraging neighbours and friends to join in communal meals across the country.

NEIGHBOURS AND communities across the United Kingdom are invited to share food and fun together at Coronation Big Lunches from Saturday 6 May to Monday 8 May 2023, in a nationwide act of celebration and friendship.

From a cup of tea with a neighbour to a street party, a Coronation Big Lunch brings the celebrations to your neighbourhood and is a great way to get to know your community a little better. The Coronation Big Lunch will be overseen and organised by the Big Lunch team at the Eden Project.

The Big Lunch is an idea from the Eden Project, made possible by The National Lottery, that brings millions of people together every year to boost community spirit, reduce loneliness and support charities and good causes. Her Majesty Queen Camilla has been Patron of The Big Lunch since 2013.

Thousands of events are expected to take place in every corner of the United Kingdom this May as people take to their streets, gardens, parks and community spaces to join the Coronation celebrations and mark this historic occasion. Free downloadable resources will also be available online at *CoronationBigLunch.com*, to help people and communities start their Coronation Big Lunch planning. ✦

To His Majesty The King and Her Majesty The Queen Consort, congratulations on your Coronation.

We are proud to serve you.
From everyone at Jack Barclay Bentley.

Jack Barclay Bentley, Berkeley Square, Mayfair, London, W1J 6AE

Emissions statement: Continental GT Azure (V8) WLTP drive cycle: fuel consumption, mpg (l/100km) – Combined 23.3 (12.1). Combined CO_2 Emissions – 275 g/km.

JACK BARCLAY

Lend a hand. Make a change.

THE BIG HELP OUT

The Big Help Out gives everyone an opportunity to join in.

THE BIG HELP OUT will be held on Monday 8 May 2023 and is being organised by The Together Coalition and a wide range of partners such as the Scouts, the Royal Voluntary Service and faith groups from across the United Kingdom. The Big Help Out will highlight the positive impact volunteering has on communities across the nation.

In tribute to His Majesty The King's public service, The Big Help Out will encourage people to try volunteering, and join the work being undertaken to support their local areas.

The aim of The Big Help Out is to use volunteering to bring communities together and create a lasting volunteering legacy from the Coronation Weekend.

From rolling up your sleeves to help a local group to joining some of the UK's leading national charities, The Big Help Out is your chance to get involved. So mark 8 May in your calendar and visit the website to discover a variety of ways in which you can lend a hand in your neighbourhood on the day.

Many of the UK's best-known charities have signed up, and more are joining each day. Whether the organisation you represent is national, regional or local, you are welcome to join in. ✦

To find out more about getting involved, please visit: **thebighelpout.org.uk**

Above: The Queen meets volunteers and citizens at the Cornhill Centre, a hub run by the Royal Voluntary Service that helps older people to stay active in their communities, in January 2020.

THE CORONATION CHAMPIONS AWARDS

In honour of Their Majesties' service to the country, the Royal Voluntary Service has launched the Coronation Champions Awards for volunteers.

TOGETHER WITH Her Majesty Queen Camilla, the awards celebrate extraordinary volunteers across the country who have been contributing to their communities.

Her Majesty said: 'I am delighted to be launching the Coronation Champions Awards with the Royal Voluntary Service, to shine a light on the herculean efforts of our nation's volunteers. Up and down the country, millions of unsung heroes are contributing to their local communities, giving generously of their time and their talents to enhance the lives of others.'

The Coronation Champions Awards will recognise a diverse group of volunteers from different backgrounds and communities across the UK from a range of causes.

Nominations closed on 2 April, and will be reviewed by an expert judging panel of volunteering specialists, charity leaders and academics. A total of 500 volunteers will be chosen as Coronation Champions and will receive a specially designed, official Coronation Champions pin and a signed certificate from His Majesty The King and Her Majesty The Queen.

All 500 Coronation Champions will also be invited to attend one of the official Coronation celebrations, such as the Coronation Concert at Windsor Castle or a Coronation Garden Party. ✦

For more information, please visit: **royalvoluntaryservice.org.uk**

Above: The Queen, President of the Royal Voluntary Service, and Elaine Paige OBE (right), pushing the snacks trolley with John Thompson (left), at the launch of the Big Trolley Push campaign at Leicester General Hospital in February 2020.

29

JENSON BUTTON

HACKETT LONDON CONGRATULATES THEIR MAJESTIES ON THE OCCASION OF THEIR CORONATION

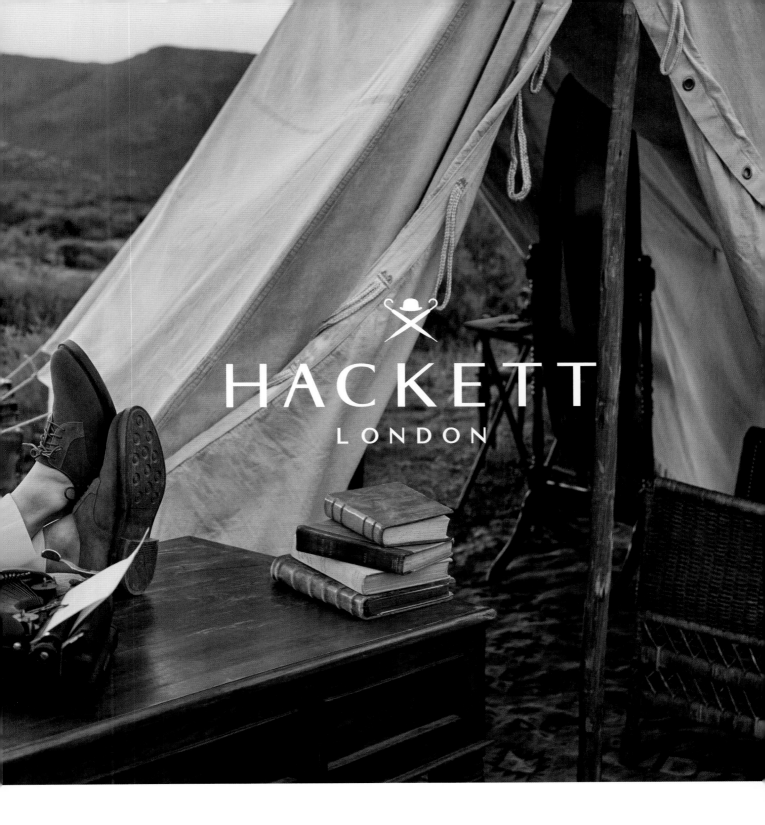

Limited-edition pocket squares are available in selected stores to celebrate this historic occasion, with all proceeds donated to a charity of HM The King's choice.

32

THE CORONATION OF HIS MAJESTY KING CHARLES III AND HER MAJESTY QUEEN CAMILLA

THE CORONATION SERVICE

INTRODUCTION FROM THE ARCHBISHOP OF CANTERBURY

The Coronation ceremony is a moment of crowning – but it also something more: it is a Christian ceremony in which the monarch makes promises to God and to the people they serve. The Archbishop of Canterbury, Justin Welby, will conduct the service.

33

Justin Welby,
Archbishop of
Canterbury.

Opposite:
Geoffrey Francis Fisher,
then Archbishop of
Canterbury, crowns
Queen Elizabeth II
at her coronation
ceremony in 1953.

CORONATIONS ARE WONDERFUL celebrations. In the history of the world, they often carry within them the hopes and prayers of nations for peace, justice and the common good. In Britain, the shape we give to coronations is a Christian service of prayer that expresses the hopes of the people, and the duties of The new King. It is a celebration with deep significance. What we hope for together – as people of many faiths and none, in this country and beyond – is held in the words and symbolism of the day. The service seals a three-way promise, between The King, the people and God.

The magnificence and pomp speak of the importance of the occasion. Yet in the midst of this glorious spectacle is a moment of stillness and simplicity. The King is anointed with oil, a symbol of being commissioned by the people for a special task for which God's help is needed. The anointing is the only part of the ceremony the public will not see. It is a private moment between a new King and the King of Kings. It is a moment when The King is set apart for service: service of the people of this country, and service of God. This is why at this moment he will exchange robes of status and honour for a simple white shirt. He will come before God, as a servant first, in the full knowledge that the task is difficult and he needs help. In the full knowledge that even as King, he is one of the people – and that even if he has a particular role to fulfil, he shares in our human frailties and vulnerabilities. In its simplicity, the anointing is the only route towards bearing power and responsibility well: asking for God's help in the task and accepting its responsibility.

As the service moves towards the moment of crowning, the mood turns to celebration as hopes, prayers and dreams are placed before God. Crowning is not the end of the service however, as The King and The Queen then receive Communion – in remembrance of Jesus Christ who laid down his life in service to us all.

My prayer for The King and The Queen, and for all those gathered in the Abbey and watching around the nation and beyond, would be that we all share the same sense of joining together before God, the King of Kings, who cares for the welfare and wellbeing of all the peoples of the Earth. ✦

THE STORY OF
WESTMINSTER ABBEY

As the venue for historic coronations and modern-day Royal Weddings, the history of Westminster Abbey is inextricably linked to that of the monarchy.

34

The Royal Wedding of The Prince and Princess of Wales, on 29 April 2011.

36

St Edward's tomb in the chapel dedicated to him at the heart of Westminster Abbey.

WESTMINSTER ABBEY has been the scene of the coronation of 39 sovereigns, each one a page in the history of the British monarchy. The first authenticated coronation was that of William I in December 1066, a ceremony commemorated in the Bayeux Tapestry which, as French legend has it, was created by William's wife Matilda. William was Duke of Normandy and was presented to the nobility of England by Aldred, the Archbishop of York, speaking in English, and Bishop Geoffrey of Coutances, speaking in French.

The names of those that have been crowned in Westminster Abbey since then resonate across the years: among them Henry VIII, Elizabeth I, Charles II, Victoria and Elizabeth II. His Majesty King Charles III will join the list on 6 May.

Westminster Abbey has also become the setting for Royal Weddings. Princess Patricia of Connaught chose Westminster Abbey for her

Westminster Abbey was also the scene of The then Princess Elizabeth's and the Duke of Edinburgh's marriage in 1947, making her the 11th member of the Royal Family to be married there.

marriage to the Hon Alexander Ramsay in 1919 – the first time in over 500 years that it had been used for a Royal Wedding, and the first since Richard II's marriage. Westminster Abbey was also chosen for the marriage of King George V's daughter Mary, the Princess Royal, to Viscount Lascelles in 1922 and that of the Duke of York to Lady Elizabeth Bowes-Lyon in 1923.

Westminster Abbey was also the scene of The then Princess Elizabeth's and The Duke of Edinburgh's marriage in 1947, making her the 11th member of the Royal Family to be married there. More recently, The Prince and >

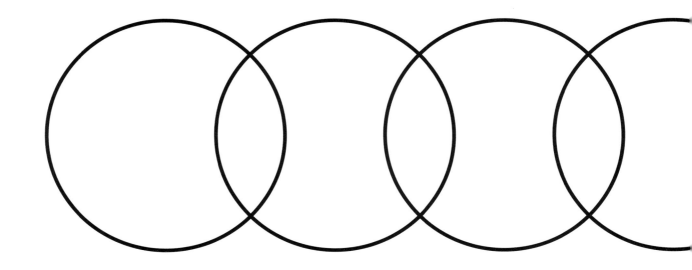

Celebrating Their Majesties
on their Coronation.

With heartfelt affection from Audi.

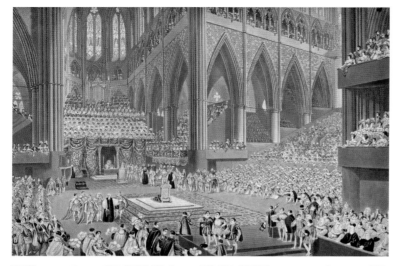

KING EDWARD'S CHAIR

The Coronation Chair, also known as King Edward's Chair, is the chair in which the sovereign is seated during the moment of crowning. It is permanently kept in Westminster Abbey. Made for Edward I, it has been used at every coronation since 1308.

After the end of the English Civil War, it was taken to Westminster Hall for the installation of Oliver Cromwell as Lord Protector in 1653. The chair was also used by Queen Victoria at her 1887 Golden Jubilee service. During the Second World War it was evacuated to Gloucester Cathedral.

The Coronation Chair was originally decorated with coloured glass, gilded with gold leaf and painted by Edward I's Master Painter. Seven centuries after it was first used, the chair is still revealing its secrets. A paintings conservator at Westminster Abbey has found evidence of previously undiscovered toes, part of the punch-work gilding on the back, that may be part of a figure.

38

Princess of Wales chose Westminster Abbey for their wedding ceremony in April 2011.

Westminster Abbey was founded on Holy Innocent's Day, 28 December 1065, when Edward the Confessor's church dedicated to St Peter was consecrated. The Confessor was buried before the High Altar, but after his canonisation in 1161, the new saint was transferred to a shrine prepared by Henry II. In 1269, his body was interred in an even more splendid shrine ordered by Henry III, who was responsible for rebuilding Westminster Abbey in the French Gothic style.

Henry VIII gave Westminster Abbey cathedral status during the Reformation, but Mary Tudor restored the Benedictine monastery in 1556. Elizabeth I founded the present Collegiate Church in 1560. The only ›

Top: An illustration of George IV's coronation, 19 July 1821.

Above: William the Conqueror's coronation features in the Bayeux Tapestry from circa 1077.

Many congratulations to His Majesty The King
and Her Majesty The Queen Consort
on their Coronation Day.

Barbour.

barbour.com

His Majesty The King speaks at the Commonwealth Day Service at Westminster Abbey in March 2023.

An architectural masterpiece, Westminster Abbey remains a huge tourist attraction, drawing visitors from all over the world, fascinated by its architecture, history and royal associations.

traces of Edward the Confessor's monastery to be seen today are in the round arches and massive supporting columns of the Undercroft in the Cloisters.

Little remains of the original medieval stained glass, once one of Westminster Abbey's chief glories, although some 13th-century panels can be seen in The Queen's Diamond Jubilee Galleries. The great west window and the rose window in the north transept date from the early 18th century, but the remainder of the glass is from the 19th century onwards. The newest stained glass is in The Queen's Window designed by David Hockney.

The last part of Westminster Abbey to be completed were the West Towers in the 18th century.

An architectural masterpiece, Westminster Abbey remains a huge tourist attraction, drawing visitors from all over the world, fascinated by its architecture, history and royal associations.

A total of 17 monarchs and 11 consorts are buried in Westminster Abbey. The tombs of our kings and queens stand not far from the memorials to our literary giants, great musicians and scientists. And it is still a church dedicated to regular worship and the celebration of great events. Special services include a Commonwealth Day service and a thanksgiving for victory in the Battle of Britain. ✦

Above, left: The West Towers of Westminster Abbey.

Top: The Queen's Window, designed by David Hockney.

Above: The Battle of Britain Memorial Window, designed by Hugh Easton.

CONGRATULATIONS YOUR MAJESTIES
ON YOUR
CORONATION
FROM
M&S

THE CORONATION OF
HM KING CHARLES III

BOODLES
1798

A FAMILY STORY

Yasmin and Amber Le Bon wear Raindance

MOMENTS
OF MAJESTY

Let us look back at some of the previous coronations, grand occasions punctuated by many memorable moments, innovations and occasional mishaps.

44

**CHARLES
II**

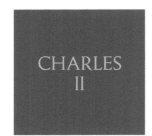

Above: In this etched illustration of the interior of Westminster Abbey, Charles II appears twice, both at the moment of crowning and afterwards, towards the front, wearing the crown before the gathered crowds.

CHARLES II RODE into London on 29 May 1660, his 30th birthday, to reclaim his crown after a long exile in Holland. Greeted with popular acclaim by a nation weary of Oliver Cromwell's draconian rule, he declared: 'I have come into my own again.'

But before he could be crowned, a new set of regalia had to be made, as Cromwell, who as Lord Protector was the head of state, had ordered the melting down of the originals.

Charles's coronation, which took place on 23 April 1661, was the last time the traditional procession of a monarch from the Tower of London to Westminster Abbey took place.

›

This powerful painting of Charles II in the Throne Room at the Palace of Holyroodhouse in Edinburgh presents an enduring image of monarchy restored. Charles is dressed in Parliament robes over the Order of the Garter costume, wearing the Crown of State, the Sword of State and the Garter Collar with the Great George, and holding the new orb and sceptre made for his coronation. The King is shown seated under a canopy of state embroidered with the royal arms, in front of an armorial cloth of honour, with a tapestry depicting the abduction of Romulus and Remus partially visible behind.

KING GEORGE V

ELIZABETH I

THE CORONATION OF GEORGE V in 1911 was remarkable because it saw the last mass gathering of European royalty before their countries became embroiled in the First World War. By the end of the war in 1918 most of them had lost their thrones, including Germany's Kaiser, The King's cousin.

The coronation, with its congregation of 6,000 people, was a splendid occasion. The first of three processions left Buckingham Palace early in the morning. The foreign royals and their representatives occupied 14 carriages. The second procession of five state landaus was for members of the British Royal Family. The third procession was for the Officers of State. The 25th and final carriage, the Gold State Coach, carried The King and Queen Mary.

At the end of the return procession, from Westminster Abbey to Buckingham Palace, there was an unexpected innovation: the appearance of The King and The Queen on the Palace balcony. This created such excitement that the soldiers outside Buckingham Palace broke ranks and joined the cheering crowd.

THE 25-YEAR-OLD QUEEN was crowned in 1559 and might have wondered how she had reached such an exalted position. Her early years had been turbulent to say the least. She was declared illegitimate after the execution of her mother, Anne Boleyn, but reinstated in the line of succession after Henry VIII's final three marriages had failed to produce children. She went on to become one of England's most celebrated monarchs.

On the day before her coronation, she made her royal entry into London with a state procession from the Tower of London through the city. The houses along the way were all decorated and the route lined with the City Guildsmen together with hundreds of flags and banners. The whole procession consisted of 1,000 horses. The Queen was carried on a litter covered in cloth of gold and lined with pink satin.

On the coronation morning she walked from Westminster Hall to Westminster Abbey in procession, flanked by the Earls of Pembroke and Shrewsbury, her train carried by the Duchess of Norfolk. She was followed by other nobles carrying the Coronation Swords, the orb and three crowns, all accompanied by the choir of the Chapel Royal. Westminster Abbey was decorated with tapestries depicting the Acts of the Apostles and scenes from Genesis. She was acclaimed by the nobility of England as their 'most undoubted Queen'.

Elizabeth did, however, find that the holy oil used to anoint her resembled grease that 'smelt ill'.   →

KING EDWARD VII

THE SON OF QUEEN VICTORIA and Prince Albert was crowned in 1902. The ceremony had moments verging on farce. The Archbishop of Canterbury's prayers were printed in large letters on cards, but he still misread some of them. And at the moment of crowning, he dropped the crown, and then placed it on The King's head the wrong way round. The King's reaction to these mishaps has not been recorded.

QUEEN VICTORIA

QUEEN VICTORIA'S CORONATION on 2 June 1838 was beset by mishaps. No one except the 19-year-old Queen seemed to know what was happening and how to do it. The Coronation Ring was painfully forced onto the wrong finger, a peer fell down the steps while making his homage and a confused bishop wrongly told The Queen that the ceremony was over, prompting her to walk away from the throne. She then had to return to her seat to complete the service. However, in her journal, Victoria concluded that the day was 'the proudest of my life'.

This painting by George Hayter captures the moment immediately after the crowning of Queen Victoria in Westminster Abbey.

GEORGE III

48

GEORGE III and Queen Charlotte were crowned on 22 September 1761, two weeks after they were married in the Chapel Royal at St James's Palace. They travelled from the Palace to Westminster Hall in sedan chairs, then walked to Westminster Abbey. The six-hour coronation service was followed by a banquet that finally ended at 10 o'clock at night.

CORONATION ROBE OF GEORGE III
This replica of the coronation robe worn by George III has a mantle of red velvet and ermine, and is shown here with the insignia of the Order of the Garter and replica waistcoat and breeches. The robe was made by Ede & Ravenscroft, and was created using 36 yards of crimson velvet and decorated with 116 yards of broad gold lace. The original robe was made of cloth of gold.

GEORGE IV

GEORGE IV'S CORONATION on 19 July 1821 was an extravaganza. The King had a new crown set with 12,000 diamonds specially made for the occasion. His estranged wife Caroline tried to gain access to the ceremony, but the door was guarded by prizefighters hired by The King to keep her out.

This coronation portrait of George IV was painted by Sir Thomas Lawrence in 1821 and records the extraordinary robes designed by The King himself. It was painted to hang in the throne room at St James's Palace, where it hangs to this day.

49

KING GEORGE VI

GEORGE VI BECAME The King unexpectedly following the abdication of his brother, King Edward VIII, in December 1936.

The coronation of The King and his consort, Queen Elizabeth, in 1937 was the last enactment of pageantry before Europe was once again plunged into war. The King and Queen's daughters, Princess Elizabeth and Princess Margaret, attended wearing robes and lightweight coronets.

The young Elizabeth recorded her thoughts at the time in an exercise book, which is now preserved in the Royal Archives at Windsor Castle. The book's cover is inscribed in red crayon with the words 'The Coronation 12th of May;

1937: to Mummy and Papa in Memory of their Coronation. From Lilibet by Herself.'

She describes the procession down The Mall to Westminster Abbey and the walk up the aisle before she went up into the Royal Box with Queen Mary. Then, as she wrote, 'The service began. I thought it all very, very wonderful; and I expect the Abbey did too. The arches and beams at the top were covered with a sort of haze of wonder as Papa was crowned, at least I thought so. When Mummy was crowned, and all the peeresses put on their coronets it looked wonderful to see arms and coronets hovering in the air, and then the arms disappear as if by magic.'

50

This formal portrait of King George VI and his family was taken immediately after his coronation by Dorothy Wilding, the first woman to be appointed as an official royal photographer.

QUEEN ELIZABETH II

THE CORONATION of Queen Elizabeth II on 2 June 1953 was one of the world's first great events to be televised, with more than half the British population tuning in to watch, along with hundreds of thousands watching across the Commonwealth. Four-year-old Prince Charles was present in Westminster Abbey, standing in the Royal Box between The Queen Mother and Princess Margaret.

Queen Elizabeth II and the Duke of Edinburgh drove back to Buckingham Palace through a canyon of cheers. In the Picture Gallery, they posed for Cecil Beaton, the country's most celebrated photographer. He found The Queen to be 'cool, smiling, sovereign of the situation', but she was looking weary after wearing the crown for three hours. 'Yes,' she remarked, 'It does get heavy.'

She would go on to reign for 70 years, longer than any other British monarch. ✦

Cecil Beaton's official photograph of Queen Elizabeth II on her coronation day, posed against a backdrop depicting the interior of Westminster Abbey. The Queen is seated facing left and looks towards the camera, wearing the Imperial State Crown. She holds the Sovereign's Sceptre in her right hand and the Sovereign's Orb in her left. She is wearing the embroidered and beaded Coronation Dress designed by Norman Hartnell and the purple velvet Coronation Robe of Estate edged with ermine.

GOD SAVE
THE KING

The dedication King Charles III brought to more than fifty years of public service as Heir to the Throne continues with the same vigour as he assumes new responsibilities as sovereign.

KING CHARLES succeeded to the throne after more than five decades of public service, having sought knowledge and inspiration from every corner of life and from everyone he has had the privilege of meeting.

Throughout his time as The Prince of Wales, His Majesty saw his purpose as supporting The late Queen Elizabeth II as the focal point for national pride, unity and allegiance. By bringing together people across all sections of society, fostering stability and continuity, highlighting achievement, protecting the country's enduring traditions and promoting tolerance and greater understanding between communities and faiths, His Majesty has led by example.

While Prince of Wales, His Majesty immersed himself in a wide variety of topics, including housing, agriculture, education, the environment, the arts, health, faith, and the well-being of rural communities.

While Prince of Wales, His Majesty immersed himself in a wide variety of topics, including housing, agriculture, education, the environment, the arts, health, faith, and the well-being of rural communities.

The King's focus has always been on the international as well as the local: for many years he has helped raise awareness of climate change and its impact on Commonwealth nations in particular. Closer to home, he took up the cause on behalf of beleaguered village pubs when he learnt that they were closing at an increasing rate. His Majesty saw difficulties and focused on solutions, encouraging pubs to become village hubs by bringing in postal services and local shops for residents.

His Majesty has had a lifelong passion for reading, opera, architecture and scholarship – and the people responsible for their creation. Valuing living traditions, he has maintained a wide circle of friends and acquaintances, ranging from childhood contemporaries, intellectuals and leading businesspeople to leading figures from the arts and the theatre.

Over the years, His Majesty has maintained a close association with hundreds of charitable patronages, bringing practical help and support wherever he can.

>

King Charles, then The Prince of Wales, poses for an official portrait to mark his 70th birthday in the gardens of Clarence House, with The then Duchess of Cornwall, The then Duke and Duchess of Cambridge, Prince George, Princess Charlotte, Prince Louis, and The Duke and Duchess of Sussex, on 5 September 2018.

54

The King during a July 2022 visit to meet young people from Morecambe, Lancashire, who have taken part in Team, a programme which helps to develop confidence, leadership and employability skills.

THE PRINCE'S TRUST

ONE OF HIS MAJESTY'S greatest contributions to social welfare was the initiation of The Prince's Trust in 1976. After completing his duty in the Royal Navy, The then Prince of Wales was determined to help improve the lives of marginalised young people. Using his Royal Navy severance pay to fund community initiatives, he laid the groundwork for the work of The Prince's Trust.

In the 47 years of its existence, The Prince's Trust has helped more than a million young people in the UK alone, with more supported overseas in recent years. Today, the charity is helping young people to develop skills and confidence to overcome barriers and build brighter futures for themselves across the UK and in more than 20 other countries.

Across the Commonwealth and beyond, the Trust supports some of the hardest to reach young people including from indigenous communities. This support includes practical assistance to tackle unemployment, poverty or health challenges, including those

Today, the charity is helping young people to develop the skills and confidence to overcome barriers and build brighter futures for themselves across the UK and in more than 20 other countries.

engaging in rehabilitation programmes.

One recent example is Olivia, whose support from The Prince's Trust helped her to overcome mental health challenges and a disrupted education. She is now thriving in employment as a healthcare worker for the NHS. Another is Ekalale Susan from Kenya whose family lost their income during the pandemic. After receiving Prince's Trust training, she set up a food stall which supports her family including her siblings' education costs. There are many other examples of those who have broken a cycle of joblessness, depression or homelessness with the charity's support.

The impact of this work goes beyond the young people themselves; it also benefits their families and wider communities, all over the world. The achievements of the young people are a testament to The King's vision and steadfast belief that all young people, everywhere, have the potential to succeed.

>

56

In November 2022, King Charles III was officially appointed to the role of The Ranger of Windsor Great Park, 70 years after The Duke of Edinburgh was first appointed to the post.

'As the enormity of the climate challenge dominates people's conversations, from newsrooms to living rooms, and as the future of humanity and nature herself are at stake, it is surely time to set aside our differences and grasp this unique opportunity to launch a substantial green recovery by putting the global economy on a confident, sustainable trajectory and, thus, save our planet.'

HIS MAJESTY THE KING AHEAD OF THE COP26
CLIMATE SUMMIT IN GLASGOW, SCOTLAND IN 2021

57

Above: The King talks with a genocide victim during his visit to the Mybo reconciliation village in Nyamata, Rwanda, in June 2022. *Left:* In November 2008, The King pays his respects to members of the Commonwealth who died during the Second World War in Jakarta. *Far left:* The King meets athletes from Wales during the 2022 Commonwealth Games in Birmingham.

AROUND THE WORLD

THE KING IS HEAD of the Commonwealth, a position he holds with pride. His predecessors as Head were Queen Elizabeth II and her late father, King George VI, though the role is not hereditary. In 2018, the Leaders of Commonwealth nations formally chose His Majesty as the next Head of this free association of 56 independent member nations, which span the globe and together are home to one-third of the world's population, including 1.5 billion people under the age of thirty.

This remarkable youth population holds what The King has described as 'extraordinary potential' for the future, as the Commonwealth member nations work towards common goals and together promote democracy

The vision is, as His Majesty puts it, for a 'Commonwealth that not only stands together, but strives together, in restless and practical pursuit of the global common good'.

and peace. The vision is, as His Majesty puts it, for a 'Commonwealth that not only stands together, but strives together, in restless and practical pursuit of the global common good'.

This Coronation year also marks the tenth anniversary of the Commonwealth Charter, which expresses the defining values of peace and justice; tolerance, respect and solidarity; care for the environment; and care for the most vulnerable. Shared values, including promoting action to combat climate change and biodiversity loss, youth education, global health and economic co-operation remain at the heart of the Commonwealth mission.

Their Majesties
The King and The Queen,
photographed by Hugo
Burnand in the grounds of
Clarence House in 2018.

60

Her Majesty Queen Elizabeth II, King Charles III (then The Prince of Wales), The Prince of Wales (then The Duke of Cambridge) and Prince George at Buckingham Palace in 2020.

A VOICE FOR THE PEOPLE

FROM THE IMPACT of climate change on communities across the world, to opportunities for young innovators, His Majesty's focus has always been on helping to find solutions for the people at the heart of national and international challenges. His Majesty makes time to fulfil his formal duties, while remaining dedicated to improving the lives of others wherever he can.

The then Prince of Wales founded The Prince's Countryside Fund in 2010 to help empower family farms and rural communities to tackle the challenges of the present and thus ensure a better future. The fund has invested millions of pounds into many hundreds of projects working across the UK to improve services in rural areas, support farming businesses and rural enterprises, and educate the next generation of young farmers.

As well as supporting communities of today, His Majesty is concerned with building the communities of tomorrow. At a virtual awards ceremony for young designers in 2020, he stated that 'it is vital that we engage with the knowledge of the past in informing not just the preservation of our historic built environment, but also the creation of sustainable, harmonious new communities'.

His Majesty's dedication to people and to society will remain constant.

The King has always cared about the impact of our surroundings and living conditions on our general well-being, helping to bring the voices of the marginalised into the mainstream. His Majesty has sought to demonstrate the value of masterplanning new communities, by sitting down with residents and respecting their knowledge about how they wish to live. He has put theory into practice in the building of new towns, including Poundbury in Dorset and Nansledan in Cornwall.

The King also devotes significant time to supporting Armed Services Personnel, including helping to ensure their work in highly dangerous circumstances receives wider appreciation.

After The King's Coronation, the pressures on His Majesty's diary will continue to be great. The royal calendar will remain exceptionally busy: receiving the Prime Minister in weekly Audience; the presentation of Credentials by incoming Ambassadors; the appointment of Bishops and Judges; visits at home and abroad and hosting Heads of State at the request of the Government. His Majesty's dedication to people and to society will remain constant. ✦

Left: The King meets with members of the UK, Commonwealth and Combined Maritime Forces at Mina Salman Naval Base, Bahrain, in 2016. *Right:* The King greets local schoolchildren during a visit to the Guru Nanak Gurdwara in Luton in 2022.

THE CORONATION OF HIS MAJESTY KING CHARLES III AND HER MAJESTY QUEEN CAMILLA

QUEEN CAMILLA

Queen Camilla supports her husband, The King, in his work and role as monarch, as well as championing a number of causes and issues close to her own heart — from childhood literacy to women's empowerment.

Her Majesty during a visit to the STORM Family Centre in London, in February 2023.

Queen Camilla with guests at a reception to celebrate British east- and
south-east Asian communities, at Buckingham Palace in February 2023.

Opposite: The King and The Queen during a visit to Brick Lane in east London in February 2023, to
meet with charities and businesses at the heart of the British Bangladeshi community.

QUEEN CAMILLA is Patron or President of over 100 charities. Her Majesty is recognised as a champion of literacy in the UK and internationally. As a grandmother, Her Majesty understands the joy of reading, but also the importance of literacy in creating opportunities later in life. Her Majesty has, over the years, visited many schools and libraries, as well as workplace reading schemes and prisons, to see the work of adult literacy schemes.

As Vice-Patron of the Royal Commonwealth Society, Her Majesty supports its flagship literacy project, The Queen's Commonwealth Essay Competition. In January 2021, Her Majesty launched her own book club on Instagram, The Queen's Reading Room, which recently became a charity in its own right, promoting an appreciation of literature.

For over a decade, The Queen has sought to highlight the work of organisations supporting victims of rape and sexual assault, undertaking numerous visits to learn more about the issues, meet survivors, and highlight the invaluable contribution made by the people and organisations working to support them. As part of this, in 2015 Her Majesty developed a project that provides washbags to victims of sexual violence after their forensic examination.

Her Majesty has also, for many years, drawn attention to the work of domestic abuse charities and the support they provide to victims and survivors, both in the UK and overseas, with the aim of breaking the taboo around the subject. In 2022, Her Majesty called on the international community to unite 'to confront what has, rightly, been called a global pandemic of violence against women'.

Other causes close to Her Majesty's heart include raising awareness of osteoporosis, and supporting those affected by diabetes and cancer. Her Majesty takes a keen and active interest in her military affiliations, which cover all three services (the Army, Navy and RAF). Her father, Major Bruce Shand, served with the 12th Royal Lancers during the Second World War, including at El Alamein, and was a prisoner of war. Her Majesty also works to promote animal welfare and has a passion for horses and dogs. In 2017, she adopted two Jack Russell terriers, Beth and Bluebell, from Battersea Dogs and Cats Home.

In addition to her work in these areas, Queen Camilla is always delighted to recognise the staff and volunteers who contribute so much to society. In her role as President of the Royal Voluntary Service, Her Majesty has backed a new scheme to honour 'unsung heroes' who volunteer to help their communities. This year, the public has been nominating inspiring volunteers for one of 500 Coronation Champions awards, so look out for the winners.

Her Majesty The Queen, President of the Women of the World Festival, hosts a Buckingham Palace reception to celebrate International Women's Day on 8 March 2023.

Above: Queen Camilla smiles with survivors, guests and photographer Allie Crewe, at Crewe's exhibition of portraits of domestic abuse survivors in Manchester, May 2022.

Above: Her Majesty visiting the annual ICAP Charity Day in London in December 2018.

Above: Her Majesty with Sawooly Li at a reception for winners of The Queen's Commonwealth Essay Competition, held at Buckingham Palace in November 2022.

Above: Queen Camilla with runner-up Amaal Fawzi at The Queen's Commonwealth Essay Competition awards ceremony at Buckingham Palace, November 2022.

Above: Her Majesty with Zahra Hussain, senior winner of The Queen's Commonwealth Essay Competition, at Buckingham Palace in 2018.

Above: Queen Camilla stands with staff holding a picture of a colleague who passed away, during a February 2022 visit to Bath-based charity VOICES. Her Majesty met people with lived experience of domestic abuse to understand how the charity works with survivors and overcomers of abuse on their journey of recovery.

Above: Queen Camilla with local school children taking part in a quiz at the Emirates Stadium in London, January 2012.

Above: Her Majesty shares a joke with Abhijit Aroia at the Cavendish Primary School in Chiswick, where she made a donation to a campaign to fund 10 reading volunteers.

Above: Queen Camilla meets Mala Breeze and her dog Flora during a reception for the 160th Anniversary of the Battersea Dogs and Cats Home animal welfare charity at Clarence House on July 14, 2022, in London.

Above: Her Majesty with Elaine Paige OBE (*left*), and Felicity Kendal (*right*) during a reception to celebrate the launch of the Royal Voluntary Service's 'Our Amazing People' campaign, at Clarence House, London, in 2022.

Right: Her Majesty chats with a young student during an event for The Queen's Commonwealth Essay Competition and Book Aid International, to learn about their work in Rwanda, at Kigali Public Library, 2022.

Left: Her Majesty at Fortnum & Mason's flagship Piccadilly store in April 2015, launching her own range of royal honey. A limited batch of 250 jars were exclusively stocked with 100% of proceeds donated to the Medical Detection Dogs charity.

Above: Her Majesty talks with D-Day veterans during lunch at a community centre in Ranville, Normandy, France, as part of the 70th anniversary of the D-Day campaign in 2014. ✦

ROYAL CONSORTS
A HISTORY

The position of royal consort to a reigning monarch of the United Kingdom may not offer constitutional power, but many consorts have made enduring contributions to national life.

THE ROLE OF A CONSORT has its roots deep in the history of the British monarchy. In medieval and Tudor times, and even later, the wife of a king was chosen for dynastic and political reasons. The young princesses from the courts of Europe often brought with them treaties, alliances and territory.

Some of our consorts have been highly influential in shaping the monarchy, despite having no constitutional position. And it is no coincidence that some of our most successful consorts have also been some of our most beloved: Prince Albert, husband of Queen Victoria; Queen Elizabeth, wife of George VI; and His Royal Highness The Prince Philip, Duke of Edinburgh, husband of Queen Elizabeth II. Here we remember some of the most notable consorts in the history of the British monarchy.

70

THE PRINCE PHILIP, DUKE OF EDINBURGH

PRINCE PHILIP was the longest-serving consort in the history of the British monarchy. His legacy is a great one. Before his retirement he had undertaken over 22,000 royal engagements at home and overseas. The late Queen Elizabeth II called him her 'strength and stay', and at the time of Her Majesty's Golden Jubilee, in 2002, she said he had made an invaluable contribution to her life. Prince Philip's description of his role was more laconic: 'All I can say is that I tried to keep it [the monarchy] going while I've been here.'

Prince Phillip came from European royalty. He was born a prince of Greece and Denmark and, because of the volatile nature of Greek politics, he lived for years in exile. When he sardonically described himself as 'a dispossessed Balkan Prince', he was telling the truth.

The Prince had a successful career in the Royal Navy and, shortly before his marriage, he renounced his Greek royal titles and became a British citizen as 'Lieutenant Philip Mountbatten RN'.

Close friends and courtiers, who worked for him over the decades, maintained that he inspired loyalty and even love.

Over the course of his life, Prince Philip was associated with 992 organisations and was a passionate advocate of many causes. He was a patron and champion of the World Wildlife Fund from its formation in 1961 until 1982, and served as the Chancellor of four universities.

However, Prince Philip is perhaps best remembered for founding the Duke of Edinburgh Award, originally designed to bridge the gap between leaving school at 15 and starting National Service at 18. Since its successful pilot in 1956, the award has supported over 8 million young people to build their confidence and life skills and now has a presence in over 130 countries and territories. The Prince's legacy lives on in the thousands of participants who continue to volunteer every year.

Close friends and courtiers, who worked for him over the decades, maintained that he inspired loyalty and even love. His biographer, Gyles Brandreth, described him as 'tolerant, kindly, amusing and amused. In several ways a man's man of his generation.' ›

Queen Elizabeth II and
The Duke of Edinburgh
photographed at the
State Opening of
Parliament in the Robing
Room of the House of
Lords on 20 June 2001.

ELEANOR OF AQUITAINE

Eleanor of Aquitaine, wife of Henry II, led armies into battle during the Second Crusade in 1147. As well as her military skill, she was known for her vast influence and political prowess. She was also a patron of the arts and she introduced the chivalric ideals of courtly love to England.

PHILIPPA OF HAINAULT

The wife of Edward III, Philippa faithfully followed and advised her husband as he made his bid for the French throne, beginning the long agony of the Hundred Years' War. She is remembered for persuading her husband not to execute the Burghers of Calais following the Siege of Calais in 1347, a story commemorated by Auguste Rodin's statue in Victoria Tower Gardens outside Parliament.

ELIZABETH OF YORK

The wife of Henry VII is regarded as the mother of the Tudor dynasty. Her marriage to Henry in 1486 ended the Wars of the Roses, uniting the Houses of York and Lancaster.

CAROLINE OF ANSBACH

The wife of George II is credited with bringing the Enlightenment to England. Intelligent and sophisticated, Queen Caroline was an important figure in helping to cement the fledgling Hanoverian dynasty from 1727 to 1737.

PRINCE ALBERT

Married to Queen Victoria at the age of 20, Prince Albert was highly protective in his role as consort and felt family life to be of great importance. Albert played a key role in organising the Great Exhibition of 1851 and popularised the use of the Christmas tree in Britain, a festive tradition that still stands today.

ELIZABETH BOWES-LYON

LADY ELIZABETH BOWES-LYON was a daughter of the Earl of Strathmore and grew up enjoying the comfortable life of the Scottish landed gentry.

In 1923 she married the Duke of York, the second son of King George V and Queen Mary. They were great favourites with the public, but in 1936, the abdication of Edward VIII propelled them into sovereignty. It was a challenge and they rose to the occasion. The next challenge was the Second World War, during which they showed themselves to be stalwart role models.

Buckingham Palace was a prime target for the German Luftwaffe and was hit nine times, prompting Queen Elizabeth to remark: 'I'm glad we've been bombed. It makes me feel I can look the East End in the face.' At the time the East End of London was under enemy attack almost every day and night. But within hours of an air raid, Queen Elizabeth was picking her way through the rubble in high heels, meeting those affected by the destruction.

While Princess Elizabeth and Princess Margaret were 'evacuated' to the relative safety of Windsor Castle, Queen Elizabeth practised firing a rifle and revolver.

'The children won't leave without me. I won't leave The King. And The King will never leave.'

'I shall not go down like the others,' she said in reference to the royal families of occupied Europe. And to suggestions that her daughters should be sent to a refuge across the Atlantic, she replied: 'The children won't leave without me. I won't leave The King. And The King will never leave.'

It is not without reason that she was described as 'The Queen of the Blitz'.

Five years later, she stood on the balcony of Buckingham Palace with The King, the princesses and the wartime Prime Minister Winston Churchill, while, below them, a surging mass of people celebrated the Allied victory.

The war was over, but it left Queen Elizabeth and King George VI drained. Sadly, in February 1952, The King died. Two days after his funeral, Queen Elizabeth made a moving pledge to the nation, saying: 'My only wish now is that I may be allowed to continue the work that we sought to do together.' It was a pledge well kept.

Consistently, she proved herself one of the most popular members of the Royal Family and an invaluable asset to her daughter, the late Queen Elizabeth II. She also became a nurturing figure to her grandson, Prince Charles, now King Charles III. ✦

72

Queen Elizabeth departs from the British Red Cross Society on 5 September 1939, with her handbag and gas mask slung over her left shoulder.

BRITISH
RED CROSS SOCIETY

73

Congratulations to Their Majesties
on this great celebration. We send

KING CHARLES III

all our good wishes for a long,
happy and glorious reign.

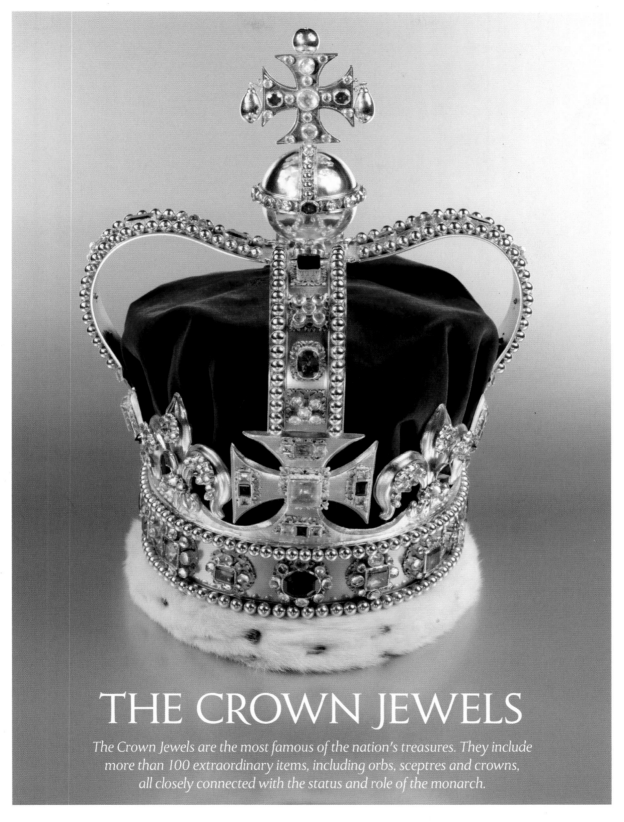

THE CROWN JEWELS

The Crown Jewels are the most famous of the nation's treasures. They include more than 100 extraordinary items, including orbs, sceptres and crowns, all closely connected with the status and role of the monarch.

ST EDWARD'S CROWN

St Edward's Crown was commissioned for the coronation of Charles II on 23 April 1661 from the Crown Jeweller, Robert Viner. The crown is composed of a solid gold frame set with semi-precious stones, including tourmalines, topazes, rubies, amethysts, sapphires, garnet, peridot, zircons, spinel and aquamarines, mounted in enamelled gold collets, and with a velvet cap with an ermine band. The band of the crown is bordered by rows of gold beads and mounted with 16 clusters, each set with a rectangular or octagonal step-cut stone in a collet decorated in enamel with modelled acanthus leaves, surrounded by rose-cut topazes and aquamarines, mainly round. At the top, the monde — which was replaced in 1685 — has similar mounts and gold beads and supports a cross-pattée, with drop-shaped beads and step-cut and rose-cut stones.

Above the band of the crown are four crosses-pattée and four fleurs-de-lis mounted with clusters of large step-cut stones and smaller rose-cut stones.

AT THE HEART of the Crown Jewels held in the Tower of London is the Coronation Regalia, a group of precious and highly symbolic objects used during every coronation ceremony since the restoration of the monarchy in 1660. Spiritually, St Edward's Crown is the most important of all the crowns on display as it is used at the exact moment of crowning.

Made of solid gold, it is decorated with 444 precious and semi-precious stones, of which there are 16 large collets in a band. The crown is formed of a circlet supporting four crosses-pattée, and four fleurs-de-lis and two intersecting arches. It is fitted with a purple velvet cap and ermine band.

The Sovereign's Orb can also be seen together with the Sovereign's Sceptre and the Imperial State Crown, which is worn by the newly crowned sovereign on their return to Buckingham Palace from Westminster Abbey.

The Crown Jewels are kept at the Tower of London. The gems, each one steeped in history, sit glistening and glittering on blue velvet, behind glass.

This is in stark contrast to the protection the jewels received during the Second World War when they were buried within the grounds of Windsor Castle, with some of the most significant diamonds hidden in a biscuit tin. ✦

The two arches are mounted with gold beads (which replace earlier rows of artificial pearls) and applied mounts with enamelled settings, containing step-cut stones and clusters of rose-cut smaller stones.

THE SOVEREIGN'S ORB

The Sovereign's Orb, a golden globe surmounted by a cross, reminds the monarch that their power is derived from God.
It is formed of a hollow gold sphere, mounted with clusters of emeralds, rubies and sapphires surrounded by rose-cut
diamonds and single rows of pearls. The cross is set with rose-cut diamonds, with a sapphire on one side
and an emerald on the other, and with pearls at the angles and at the end of each arm.

THE AMPULLA AND SPOON

The gold Ampulla or vessel is cast in the form of an eagle with outspread wings, on a domed and foliate base, and a foot chased with auricular scrolls and masks. The head of the eagle screws off, and there is an aperture in the beak for pouring the oil. The Ampulla is used to hold the consecrated chrism oil with which a sovereign is anointed during the coronation ceremony.

The design, in the form of an eagle, is based on an earlier, smaller vessel, which in turn was based on a 14th-century legend that the Virgin Mary appeared to St Thomas à Becket and presented him with a golden eagle and a vial of oil for anointing future kings of England.

Traditionally the oil is placed in the Ampulla, and then poured into the

12th-century Anointing Spoon – which survived Parliament's destruction of the Crown Jewels in 1649 – at the most sacred moment of the coronation. The gesture of anointing, when the Archbishop touches holy oil onto the head, breast and hands of the sovereign, dates back to the Old Testament Book of Kings, where the anointing of Solomon is described.

THE SOVEREIGN'S SCEPTRE WITH CROSS

The Sovereign's Sceptre comprises a gold rod, formed in three sections, with enamelled collars at the intersections, surmounted by an enamelled heart-shaped structure, which holds a drop-shaped diamond, Cullinan I, weighing 530.2 carats.

This structure is surmounted by enamelled brackets mounted with step-cut emeralds, and by a faceted amethyst monde, set with table- and rose-cut diamonds, rubies, spinels and emeralds. A cross above is set with further diamonds, with a table-cut diamond on the front, and an emerald on the reverse.

Beneath the Cullinan diamond are further enamelled brackets, representing a crown, mounted with rubies and diamonds. The pommel of the sceptre is enamelled and mounted with rubies, emeralds, sapphires and diamonds.

The sceptre represents the

sovereign's temporal power and is associated with good governance. During the coronation service the new sovereign is first anointed with holy oil, then robed in coronation robes, and then invested with a number of ornaments symbolising the chivalric nature of kingship. These include the spurs, swords and armills, followed by the orb, a ring and then the sceptres.

The sovereign is presented with two sceptres – this one surmounted by a cross and another surmounted by a dove (which represents the Holy Ghost). The investiture culminates with the crowning of the sovereign.

Originally made for Charles II, the sceptre has undergone a number of alterations since 1661, most significantly in 1910 when it was altered to receive the Cullinan diamond.

The structure which holds the diamond is hinged so that the stone may be removed and worn separately.

Celebrate with fantastic flavour

Add a pinch of Maldon Salt

For four generations we've hand-harvested our famous, pyramid-shaped flakes, using the same simple, time-honoured techniques. Fantastic flavour is at your fingertips.

EST. 1882

Maldon®

SEA SALT
FLAKES

80

IMPERIAL STATE CROWN

The Imperial State Crown was made for the coronation of King George VI in 1937, replacing a crown made for Queen Victoria. The crown is set with 2,868 diamonds, as well as with several famous jewels. It includes St Edward's Sapphire, said to have been worn in a ring by Edward the Confessor. The crown also includes the Cullinan II diamond, the second largest stone cut from the great Cullinan diamond. The Imperial State Crown is worn by the monarch when leaving Westminster Abbey after the coronation ceremony.

SAVILE ROW GIN CONGRATULATES HIS MAJESTY THE KING
AND HER MAJESTY THE QUEEN CONSORT
ON THE OCCASION OF THEIR CORONATION

42% ABV, 12 Botanicals

savilerow-gin.co.uk

THE DESCENT OF THE CROWN

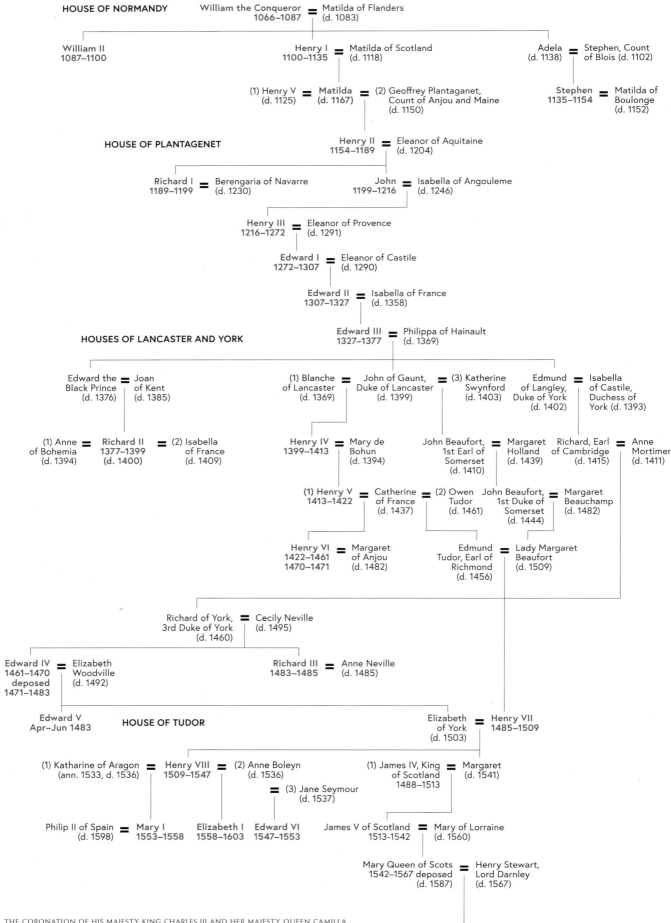

HOUSE OF NORMANDY

William the Conqueror ━ Matilda of Flanders
1066–1087 (d. 1083)

William II
1087–1100

Henry I ━ Matilda of Scotland
1100–1135 (d. 1118)

Adela ━ Stephen, Count
(d. 1138) of Blois (d. 1102)

(1) Henry V ━ Matilda ━ (2) Geoffrey Plantaganet,
(d. 1125) (d. 1167) Count of Anjou and Maine
(d. 1150)

Stephen ━ Matilda of
1135–1154 Boulonge
(d. 1152)

HOUSE OF PLANTAGENET

Henry II ━ Eleanor of Aquitaine
1154–1189 (d. 1204)

Richard I ━ Berengaria of Navarre
1189–1199 (d. 1230)

John ━ Isabella of Angouleme
1199–1216 (d. 1246)

Henry III ━ Eleanor of Provence
1216–1272 (d. 1291)

Edward I ━ Eleanor of Castile
1272–1307 (d. 1290)

Edward II ━ Isabella of France
1307–1327 (d. 1358)

HOUSES OF LANCASTER AND YORK

Edward III ━ Philippa of Hainault
1327–1377 (d. 1369)

Edward the ━ Joan
Black Prince of Kent
(d. 1376) (d. 1385)

(1) Blanche ━ John of Gaunt, ━ (3) Katherine
of Lancaster Duke of Lancaster Swynford
(d. 1369) (d. 1399) (d. 1403)

Edmund ━ Isabella
of Langley, of Castile,
Duke of York Duchess of
(d. 1402) York (d. 1393)

(1) Anne ━ Richard II ━ (2) Isabella
of Bohemia 1377–1399 of France
(d. 1394) (d. 1400) (d. 1409)

Henry IV ━ Mary de
1399–1413 Bohun
(d. 1394)

John Beaufort, ━ Margaret
1st Earl of Holland
Somerset (d. 1439)
(d. 1410)

Richard, Earl ━ Anne
of Cambridge Mortimer
(d. 1415) (d. 1411)

(1) Henry V ━ Catherine ━ (2) Owen
1413–1422 of France Tudor
(d. 1437) (d. 1461)

John Beaufort, ━ Margaret
1st Duke of Beauchamp
Somerset (d. 1482)
(d. 1444)

Henry VI ━ Margaret
1422–1461 of Anjou
1470–1471 (d. 1482)

Edmund ━ Lady Margaret
Tudor, Earl of Beaufort
Richmond (d. 1509)
(d. 1456)

Richard of York, ━ Cecily Neville
3rd Duke of York (d. 1495)
(d. 1460)

Edward IV ━ Elizabeth
1461–1470 Woodville
deposed (d. 1492)
1471–1483

Richard III ━ Anne Neville
1483–1485 (d. 1485)

Edward V
Apr–Jun 1483

HOUSE OF TUDOR

Elizabeth ━ Henry VII
of York 1485–1509
(d. 1503)

(1) Katharine of Aragon ━ Henry VIII ━ (2) Anne Boleyn
(ann. 1533, d. 1536) 1509–1547 (d. 1536)

(1) James IV, King ━ Margaret
of Scotland (d. 1541)
1488–1513

━ (3) Jane Seymour
(d. 1537)

Philip II of Spain ━ Mary I
(d. 1598) 1553–1558

Elizabeth I
1558–1603

Edward VI
1547–1553

James V of Scotland ━ Mary of Lorraine
1513-1542 (d. 1560)

Mary Queen of Scots ━ Henry Stewart,
1542–1567 deposed Lord Darnley
(d. 1587) (d. 1567)